Love's
EVOLUTION

BILLIE STEPHENS-OGDEN

BALBOA.PRESS
A DIVISION OF HAY HOUSE

Balboa Press books may be ordered through booksellers or by contacting:

Balboa Press
A Division of Hay House
1663 Liberty Drive
Bloomington, IN 47403
www.balboapress.com
844-682-1282

ISBN: 979-8-7652-3444-0 (sc)
ISBN: 979-8-7652-3445-7 (e)

Print information available on the last page.

Balboa Press rev. date: 09/21/2022

Dedication

This book is dedicated to all the people in my life who have given me the opportunity to experience one form, or other, of love.

And

To every person who will ever seek for or has ever hoped to know love.

And

With a very special dedication to Allen Ogden,
My husband of 37 years, my best friend, and lover, who helps me to always steer my life towards a pathway of gentleness and faith in God. He is the glue that helped me to put this book together.

Every person deserves someone to love and be loved by, and that begins with Self Love.

About the Author

Billie has always had some kind of connection with Spirit: From having an imaginary childhood friend called Peter, who would help her with her problems as a child, to finding some solace in God as an adult, during her less-than-ideal 20-year marriage to her first husband.

After her divorce, Billie found herself without any financial support, and had to find her own way in life. She had to walk 5-miles each way to get to work because she could not afford bus fare. She nearly starved the first six months after their breakup, as she had no money for food. She was alone, lonely, and wondered what life was about and if it had any meaning whatsoever. At times she would think about suicide, but never seriously considered it because there was a force that encouraged her to keep turning within to find answers. All she could do was live one moment at a time

She knew she needed help and began writing to God almost every night to empty her Soul of the pain and limitation she found herself in. She called it cheap therapy. She did not have a clue as to how to repair her life or her heart and figured only God could help. Billie was never a religious person but had a deep faith in God and claims that her faith in God is what saved her life.

During the course of the following years, she evolved from a victim of life to a life of self-empowerment. She discovered that all the years of a chaotic and unfulfilling marriage was a school or classroom with lessons custom-made to assist her in growing spiritually, and to take responsibility for all conditions, circumstances, and aspects of life. She now considers her former husband a master teacher who assisted her in finding her own answers to life's challenges.

In 1989 she became an ordained minister in a non-denominational church. She has become a metaphysical consultant and has clients world-wide who call her for clarity in their lives. Billie has developed her own workshops and classes in self-healing, meditation, and relationships. For 18 years she has published a monthly newsletter titled "WE R 1", where she allows Spirit to speak through it, giving messages to inspire and lovingly guide its readers.

PLEASE NOTE:

Names of all individuals mentioned in this book have been changed to protect their privacy except for her current husband, Allen Ogden.

I Don't Love Him Anymore

When I see him loving her
    I feel an emptiness inside
        Even though I don't Love him anymore.

No, I don't love him anymore!

When I hear him laugh with her
    I feel a hurt a mile wide.
        Even though I don't Love him anymore.

No, I don't love him anymore!

I look at the picture of them together
    and my eyes fill with tears,
        Even though, I don't Love him anymore.

No, I don't love him anymore!

Loneliness seems to be my reward
    for almost twenty years of devotion
        Even though, I don't Love him anymore.

No, I don't love him anymore!

Today's comment: A painful process of letting go of that which I knew prevented me from being all that I could be. Even though the pain of ending a twenty year marriage was never-the-less immeasurable, I knew I had to leave the marriage in order for me to grow.

Dedicated to my first husband: *A man who constantly demanded that I change and become what I was not. I am grateful, even though the lessons were filled with pain and heart break, they nevertheless led me toward becoming more aware of who I wanted to be. We both made much better lives for ourselves.*

I'm Lookin' For Love

I was married but lonely,
    Now, I'm single and alone.

I'm lookin' for love.

Where does one go to look for love?
    Where does one go to search?

Hello there! Are you the One?
    Are you here to take away my hurt?

I'm lookin' for love.

I'm in search of a friend, a love.
    Someone to hold my hand and walk with me.

Someone to share a moonlit night or
    A glass of wine by firelight.

I'm lookin' for love.

There must be someone who wants my love.
    Someone who can love me, too.

There must be someone, somewhere who is searchin'.
    Someone who is lookin' for me.

I'm lookin' for love.

Today's comment: The thoughts of being alone and unloved were terrifying to me at that time. I didn't know what love really was, but I knew I wanted it. I had no idea that love was found within. I just knew that love was something that should make me feel happy and good and complete.

Dedicated to: *Every woman or man who has ever believed that love is something that is outside of themselves.*

I Cry Alone

I needed you - you weren't there.
I cried alone!

Now, you come - you have a problem.
You know I'll always listen.

You scold me when you notice
I don't seem my happy self.

You tell me you care - you love me.
You must go, she is waiting.

I'm left alone - to face the world.
I cry alone.

I love you - I wait.
You belong to another.

Why? Why can't I just walk away:
Will I love you forever?

Yes! I will love you eternally,
For that is my way.

Today's comment: The limitations I accepted for a little kindness, attention, and affection were huge. This was my first relationship, after the divorce. He was a married man. He was sometimes kind and often complimentary. I had spent 38 years without these things. I would love anyone who gave them to me. I needed someone to tell me I was okay, even if it caused me pain in other areas.

Dedicated to: *The first man in my life to make me feel attractive and wanted. He always told me I should surround myself in beauty for only then could I blossom. I took his words to heart.*

What's It All About

Today, I wrote in the sand,
"What is the purpose of life?"

The waves washed it away,
as I finished the last letter.

Was that my answer?
If so, what did it mean?

Is life just a wash out?
Is there any meaning at all to life?

Was my question not worthy of being answered?
Did it mean there is no answer, so erase the question?

What is life all about?
Why am I here?

Will I ever know?
Does anyone care if I know?

Today, I have lots of questions
And no answers.

<u>Today's comment:</u>   I spent many hours walking the beaches of southern California trying to find myself and the answers to life. What I found by asking the questions, was that I had turned my feelings off for years, and now that I was allowing them to surface, I was experiencing years of pain all at once. Life felt too difficult, and I wanted to die but I couldn't take my own life, for God had given me that gift. I believed in a loving God. I just didn't believe I was lovable.

Dedicated to: *Every soul who is looking for the answers of life and of love and how they fit together in this intricate web we weave, called life.*

Our Time Together

I was older.
He was quite young.
Age didn't seem to matter.

He was on the wild side.
I was conservative.
We had so much fun together.

I tried to be young at heart.
He tried to be mature.
We filled each other's life with newness.

We tried to be friends.
We were lovers.
We promised not to fall in love.

Our affair was short.
It was intense.
We tried hard to be honest.

He went back to his life.
I went back to being alone.
We are what we are because of our time together.

Today's comment: This young man (I was 38, he was 24) made me feel alive and young and beautiful; things I had never experienced in my life. I cried when we parted, and I loved him, and I knew it was not the kind of love I was looking for.

Today, I am grateful the universe has provided me with so many people to help me find myself and to know what love truly is.

Dedicated to: *A young man (whose name I can't even remember) who made me remember how to laugh again. He taught me that while I was laughing, I couldn't cry. I didn't always remember this lesson, but when I did, it made a difference to me. Thank you!*

I'm Trying To Remember What Love Is

I wanted to love you so much.
        I clung tightly.

Then I remembered that love is freedom.
        I had to let you go.

At first, I felt a loss.
        It made me hurt inside.

Then, I remembered loss is illusion.
        Now, I feel love, again.

My love for you is unconditional
        You don't have to love me the same way.

My love for you must not be materialistic.
        We seem to be going in different directions.

Yet, my love is very strong.
        Loving you is loving me is loving God.

Today's comment: I wanted so much to love him openly and to be loved openly and our love was not equal. Was I going to love every man I met? Would I ever not love men? Yes! I finally learned that it is my way to love all, and to be selective as to how I allow that love to take form in my life. I also discovered that just because I felt love for a man did not mean I wanted romance with him. So, what was the meaning of love, after all?

Dedicated to: *Andy. I was 39 and he was 27. We laughed; I cried; I still love him. I love all the men who have helped me to learn about love. He taught me to make decisions for myself and to think about what I wanted my life to be all about.*

I Love You - Be On Your Way

I love you all the wrong ways.
I care for you, and I like you.
You've hurt me and I still love you.

You've been unkind and uncaring.
I love you; you say you care for me,
But if only I would change some parts of me.

Your love has too high of a price.
I can't afford my heart to be broken anymore.
Love is all there is - be on your way!

Today's comment: He was so critical and cynical about so many things; I was afraid of being put back into the box I had finally gotten out of. I felt pain about this, but again, I knew it was not the love I was looking for. Enough pain and I finally began to get smart even if I couldn't stop loving him.

Dedicated to: *Andy again! We did have some good moments. Through Andy I learned that I deserve to be loved as deeply as I love others.*

The Rain Of Life

The rain is falling is
upon my life.

It is the tears of
a child of God.

As they stream down
my cheeks

I wonder how many
lives they fall upon.

Today's comment: I began to seek for my connection with all others. As I did this, I discovered there were many people who did not understand love and they cried many tears too. I was learning to care about what others went through and I wanted to erase their tears, even though I was still crying.

Dedicated to: *Every person who has ever felt unloved or alone in their life. I can only promise you, that when you begin to love others exactly as they are, they will love you back, as much as they know how.*

A Transforming Perception

Feeling uncomfortable with life
    Can be painful
        and surely very difficult.

Why do we do this to ourselves?
    What causes the feeling of discomfort
        and discontent within us?

Thinking on this I realize it is
    a lack of confidence in myself.
        I feel so unsure most of the time.

I'm not sure people will accept
    me or like me, if I'm not willing
        to be what they want me to be.

Yet, I know somewhere deep inside
    of me is the woman God created,
        therefore, I must be acceptable.

Maybe that is where I need to
    start looking - inside of me -
        For that woman God created.

Maybe, just maybe, this is the answer.
    Could it be there is a pathway inside of me?
        I need to find my way in.

Today's comment: Asking questions has, again, set me off in a direction which leads to growth and understanding.

Dedicated to: *All the people of the world who are still looking outside of themselves for the answers to life.*

Am I A Who Or A What?

A who is a person.
  A mind personified.

I wish to go beyond who so,
  what does that make me?

If I am merely a person, I'd be limited,
  I don't think I am.

I am everything seen and unseen.
  So that makes me Spirit - a what.

Today's comment: Breaking through the traditional thinking of what I was, was very abstract
  and answers just brought more questions.

Dedicated to: *Every person who is trying to break with the traditional thinking they were trained
  to believe. And to each person who wants out of the box.*

What Am I Doing Wrong?

Is my body illusion?
Is it not there?

It feels so real.
Yet, I seem to rebel.

My body reacts to people.
It especially reacts to men.

When a man reaches out to me with words,
my mind reacts and becomes alive.

When he reaches out to me with hands,
My body reacts and wants to touch.

I start out *reaching* for the soul,
Yet, I somehow get caught up,

In the physical and I settle,
for the physical body.

Todays Comment: My heart knew what love was, but my body didn't have a clue. I was just beginning to learn that physical relationships do not mean love. My head had to discover the difference between my heart and my body.

Dedicated to: *Everyone who thinks a physical relationship is love.*

What Do I want?

I want to know that you will
    try to accept my love.

I want to know that you are happy,
    For only then, am I whole.

I want to know that you are ever-growing.
    never stagnant.

I want to help you find freedom
    within yourself

I want to see you at peace with yourself
    and your world.

I want to help you find truth,
    which is love.

I want to help you to overcome all fear,
    the opposite of love.

My wants are few, my demands are nonexistent.
    My love is complete, eternal.

Today's comment: I was learning to let the woman inside of me speak to the woman outside of me. I was beginning to listen to the voice of God within me. The more I did this, the broader my vision became. It still was not easy, but it had hope of fulfillment.

Dedicated to: *Everyone who has never listened to the voice within which is a great comforter and always offers love in every situation.*

I Want To Love You - As I Know How

You seemed so forlorn -
I wanted to reach out and touch you.

I wanted to share my happiness with you -
To see the smile on your face, enter your eyes.

Your smile was not real -
Your eyes spoke of unhappy times and pain.

Your voice spoke words of indifference -
Yet, I heard a cry for trust, friendship and love.

You wear a mask of uncaring-
Yet, I know you care deeply within.

You speak words of certainty -
Yet, your voice speaks of doubt.

To you, I offer a gift of universal love -
All that I am.

I am willing to accept from you all your pain and
doubt and transform them into love and happiness.

Today's comment: As I began to watch the people around me, I saw so many people who
were living what they thought they should be, instead of what they were. I
wanted to take them into my arms and cradle them and give them a place
of safety to come out of themselves. I didn't really know how to do this, I
just wanted to do it.

Dedicated to: *Every person who hides within themselves their own truth, happiness and the joy*
that is their God given right to express.

Sharing

Sharing is going beyond ourselves.
    Sharing is trusting you, with me.

To allow you to know my faults
    and imperfections see.

When you are down and needy,
    Extra strength I will find.

Yet, when it's strength I need,
    I come to you, leaving pride behind.

We talk of you. We talk of me.
    There isn't anything we can't share.

We give to and of each other,
    simply because we love and care.

Today's comment: I was writing about what I wanted a relationship to be about, in my life. Not that I was experiencing it yet, at that point. I realized I had to have clarity about what I did and did not want in a relationship before I could manifest it. I still had some growing to do.

Dedicated to: *The voice within me. It had become my greatest comforter. It was always willing to remind me of the good things about me. The more I turned to the voice within with my problems and fears, the more I discovered a wonderful friend just waiting there for me.*

I Want To Know

I want to know who I am.
        I want to know what I am.

I want to know what love is.
        I want to experience love's wholeness.

I pray to know everything there is
        to know about love.

I want my life to be about
        the truth of love.

Somehow, I know love
        is the answer.

May I please have heavenly
        help with this?

Today's comment: As I look back, I see that my desire to love was the greatest force in my life; all my growth and change came from this. I would ask for love to fill me, and I could get through anything that life seemed to throw at me.

Dedicated to: *Myself; for the continuing belief in something I was so very unsure of, yet, trusted, and for trusting the voice within and surrendering myself unto that voice of love*

To You I Give

To You I give all that I am
A giant love
A helping hand.

To you, I give all that I see
A beautiful love
For you and for me.

Through God our Father,
I give to you a love that is deep
A love that is true.

I'll give to you, and you'll give to me
A pure sweet love
of honesty.

Today's comment: The voice kept telling me that when I could feel this way about myself, I was ready for a Holy relationship instead of just a relationship filled with lessons. I wanted so much to be ready; I knew this was not something one can rush. We are all where we are when we are there, and we can't be anywhere else until we are ready.

Dedicated to: *The voice of God which lies within the heart of each of us born unto this world of lessons and discoveries and experiences.*

Dear God

Life seems full of little things we do not see
     because what seems like BIG things cover them up.

Sometimes the little things are so numerous, they
     pile up and look like a big thing.

My love for you is a BIG thing made up of the
     many little things you do for me.

Your love for me is alive through mankind's actions,
     little winks, touches, hugs, and smiles.

My life is filled with the Greatness of your
     love and the many ways you show it.

You are the flight of my heart
     And the peace of my being.

I thank you!

Today's comment: I began to see how gratitude played a very important role in a relationship. My relationship with God was now the most important thing in my life. Just because God was omnipotent did not mean He did not appreciate being appreciated. I wanted to befriend God. Little did I know that meant I had to befriend myself and others.

Dedicated to: *God. My loving Father who has never let me down, or made me wrong, or held back love, regardless of what I have ever done or not done in my life. He has always accepted me exactly as I am in any given moment.*

Panic Or Peace?

I feel as if I should be in a panic or something,
        because I haven't found work. Yet, I'm calm.

I think I should be more concerned about my future.
        Why aren't I?

The shoulda, woulda, coulda syndrome is
        trying to attack me again.

I know that the jobs I've applied for so far
        would not be fulfilling to me and I will find my place.

I want to help people to know who they are.
        I want them to know they are loved.

I want to grow, and I want to help
        others to do the same.

I want to take my place in the Truth of God,
        whatever that is.

Today's comment: The realization began to take hold, that all of God's children deserve to be loved. I also began to see that when I allowed the love of God to flow through me, I could not contain it all and therefore the more of it I gave away, the more of it I had. It is like becoming a fountain. Loving others became easy and effortless. Loving people was my salvation!

Dedication To: *That fountain of love that flows so very freely from anyone who is willing to allow it to do so. It is contagious. Everyone it flows upon will take a piece of the fountain with them and it will begin to grow within them, to whatever extent they will allow. Love is that powerful.*

My Lord

The Lord is my shepherd.
    I am His lamb.

Together, we walk
    through life in love.

My trust in Him is unconditional.
    His love for me is the same.

Together we walk
    the pathway to eternity.

He expects me to follow.
    I expect Him to lead.

Our love has become united
    in my goal of loving God.

I take His love.
    He takes my hand.

Together, we travel onward.

Today's comment: As I began to trust the Love of God, I noticed that the people around me began to change. Old acquaintances seemed to go their own way. New acquaintances entered my life. They were seeking just as I was. Support was coming from all directions.

Dedicated to: *All the people who have been in my life in one way or another, for long periods or short periods, because you have all helped to mold this woman into what she has become.*

I Am Free

I want to love.
    I want freedom.
        I want to know truth.

I am truth,
    therefore, I have the
        freedom to love.

I am love,
    therefore, I have the
        freedom to know and see truth.

I am lovingly free
    and
        I am freely loving.

I am freely truthful
    and
        I am truthfully free.

I am all that I am
    and
        I am happy.

I am content
    and
        I am free.

Today's comment: I began to discover that I could go beyond my comfort zone on paper and stretch my self-image without being threatened. Once I got it on paper, I almost always found a way to weave it into my life without as much fear. I began to expand. I began to find out who and what I am.

Dedicated to: *Every person who feels boxed in and is looking for a way out of the limitations they are experiencing in life.*

Inner Contradictions

I strive for happiness -
>Yet, part of me wants to go on crying.

I work hard for success -
>Yet, part of me insists on some failure.

I thrill at giving of myself -
>Yet, part of me wants to hold back.

I feel warmth at receiving -
>Yet, part of me feels unworthy to receive.

I pray for answers and for help -
>Yet, part of me turns a deaf ear.

I praise God as my Father -
>Yet, I shy away from being praised as His child.

I offer all my love to God, my Father -
>Yet, I'm afraid to accept His love for me.

I am a being divided -
>Yet, I know this need not be.

I want to be united with my Father,
>Yet, I fight to keep my illusions.

I want to let Spirit help me,
>Yet, I struggle on, day by day.

Today's comment: Each time I could see the difference between where I was and where I wanted to be, I would find myself in a pivotal place where I could make choices based on self-love and self-growth; they frightened me and yet I wanted nothing more. I wanted to make my own choices, yet I was afraid to make my own choices because I didn't want the responsibility of taking care of myself. Now, I know that freedom is based upon making my own decisions. Right, wrong, or in between, my decisions reflect my truth and my willingness to live that truth.

Dedicated to: *Every person who has ever struggled within themselves to find peace of mind.*

Voices

There was a whisper in my mind. At first it was just a
sound mixed with the rest of the chatter
that continuously goes on and on.

Yet, somehow, this whisper was different,
even though I could not distinguish it,
I knew it was significant to my life.
My quest for truth began.

As I learned what the whisper was not,
my life began to change with each new day.
The changes were fun, fearful and adventurous.
I began to see change as growth.

My tears cleansed me and added to my growth.
The laughter nourished me, and I blossomed.
The fear, trying to hold me back, strengthened me.
The adventure added spice to this new flower.

Now, the whisper is constantly in my mind.
It is clear and very distinct.
My minds chatter can no longer hide the words,
"I love you Billie."

Today's comment: When you seek for something from your heart, you will find it. It is important for each of us to be in touch with our own heart voice, so our lives flow instead of being filled with resistance and fear. For indeed, love and fear cannot coexist.

Dedicated to: *You, the reader. I reach out to you with words, and I hope you will allow yourself to receive the love within the words, and the embrace between the lines, and the devotion throughout the pages.*

Within

From the battle of time, I emerge
to live a life of love.

No longer to struggle for breath
but to live in the sea of peace.

Mine is a life of joy
for truth has become my vision.

Come, take my hand.
Feel the surge of life.

Listen to your whispering soul
seeking its peace in God.

Whispering gently in your mind
the voice calling you home to love.

Today's comment: Surrender is the one factor that was very necessary to move my life from fear and doubt into the heart place of love. Surrender is one of those things that is easy to want and to talk about and a lot harder to follow through on. Constant practice makes it happen.

Dedicated to: *Every person who feels the need to be in control of their own life and therefore the lives of those around them. We do not need to control; we simply need to surrender.*

Happiness

Happiness is not at the end of the rainbow.
It is the joy inside of me as
I behold the color spectrum of life.

Happiness is not having someone Love me.
It is the pleasure within,
of sharing my love with others.

Happiness is not hearing a song of the meadowlark.
It is hearing the song of peace within,
as I recognize that love is a gift from God.

Happiness is not feeling the breeze on my cheeks as I walk along.
It is having the sensitivity to recognize
God touching me through that breeze.

Happiness is not something I can get from another.
It is the contentment within
when I realize who and what I am.

Today's comment: As I discovered more about myself, the journey inward became somewhat easier. We must each map out our own journey within, considering there are no maps for the journey. I ask angels for help, constantly. The longer I stay on my journey inward, the wider and more comfortable the path gets.

Dedicated to: *All the angels and heavenly Beings who have helped me time after time and lifted my spirits when I thought it couldn't be done. I am grateful for their unconditional love. They always help, when asked*

Was He Real?

I looked up and met his eyes with mine,
I found an open channel.
As our eyes held fast - for seconds eternal,
we shared my total being.

Between us passed a knowledge that
we already knew each other well.
As he touched me with his eyes, I was aware of
a gentleness I had never seen in anyone.

The external smile lines described a happy,
well-adjusted man of gentleness.
The silent communication told me he was
looking for someone to share his being with.

The soul spoke of a loving man who had
overcome earthly pain.
He awakened within me a desire to
verbally share what we had just experienced.

I waited for him to walk across the room and touch me.
I wanted to physically feel his gentleness up close.
When his hand touched mine, I knew
I had been correct.

He knew that I knew he wanted to touch me
and I wanted to be touched by him.
The moment his hand touched mine I felt
as if the earth changed and heaven opened
a whole new world to me.

I knew it wouldn't be the last touch,
so there was no reason to rush.
I wanted to bathe warmly in each moment of discovery.
As we spoke, our eyes spoke of more meaningful things.

As he slipped his arm around
my waist as we walked,
I experienced a comfort and ease
I had never known before.
It felt like floating through space.
It felt heavenly

(continued on next page)

Was He Real? (*Continued from previous page*)

I wanted each new discovery to last a long time.
I wanted to absorb him.
When he took me home, he gently kissed me goodnight.
I did not know just a kiss could make me
feel the depth of another person

Again, I wanted each moment to last forever
because it felt heavenly. It felt so right.
It was as if I had found a part of me
that had been lost
and now I was found

There was no lust, no need,
just the meeting of two souls.
To be held, to be kissed was complete.
I couldn't have handled more.

I knew there would be other times,
we would slowly discover each other.
We will build. We will find ourselves in
each other and find wholeness.

Today's comment: I wrote this that evening, after he left me at my doorstep. I never saw this man again! It is as if he disappeared into thin air. I was not unhappy. I felt honored to have had the experience. It was such a joy to experience such sensitivity with another human, especially a man. For the first time, I realized men can be sensitive. I went back to his condo the next week. He had told me he would be away for a short time. When I got there, no one was there, and the neighbor told me no one had lived there for many months. I peeked in the window and saw it was empty. Yet, a week before I spent several hours in that fully furnished condo, with that man, talking my heart out.

Dedicated to: *The "angel" who awoke within me sensitivity I wasn't aware that I had. Through that sensitivity I reached an ever-higher level of self-awareness and self-acceptance. I thank you, "angel", though I know not whether you were a man or an angel. I suspect the latter.*

My Prayer

I prayed to understand humankind.
I experienced pain,
as they do.

I prayed to love humankind unconditionally.
I felt rejection,
as they do.

I prayed to be sensitive to humankind
I had my feelings hurt,
as they do.

I prayed to take my place in the universe
I became a teacher.

I prayed I would be a good teacher.
I became a student.

I prayed for the knowledge of truth.
I am filled with love.

I prayed to be all that I am,
so, I give me, now, to you.

Today's comment: My hunger for love became a hunger to love all of humanity equally. I wanted to love every person I met with the love I felt inside. I believed that I could do this and still have a mate. I began to understand that God's love makes no judgement, therefore, I had to work upon my own judgements, if I hoped to attain this.

Dedicated to: *The hunger for truth that lies deep within each of us and drives us forward even when we don't know what direction to go.*

My Love For All Of You

I believe the best friendships are those
     Based on openness, honesty, and freedom.

I am open enough to tell
     you I honestly love you.

I am also free enough to allow you the
     freedom to love me or not to love me.

I love you because I enjoy loving you.
     Not because I want love in return.

I love you with a gentleness
     that requires no reply.

The love I feel for you
     is the unconditional vintage of God's Love.

Today's comment: The fear of being hurt by the love of another vanishes when I love freely and openly. There is nothing to hide. I am now willing to let those I meet know the whole truth about me and they will either love me or they won't. I can't love someone openly if I am in fear they won't like or love me.

Dedicated to: *Every friend I have ever had in my life. I am so glad you were there, even if it wasn't all roses. I know we all did the best we could to be the best we could.*

The Flow Of Love

I am a fountain of love
I pour fourth all that I am.

As long as there is someone reaching out,
My love shall flow, touching all in reach.

My love flows freely to all
Who stop and care to receive.

Please don't refuse my love
With closed hearts and uncaring minds.

Receive my love, enjoy it.
Then give it to a friend.

Accept even more of my love
Then share it with the world.

Today's comment: I asked to have an experience of what love was and this writing came forth. These words went through my mind over and over. I believe God put them there and I learned the more love I am willing to give away, the more love that comes into my life. Love seems to be an amazing energy that just grows and grows when given away. When I am upset with someone and I take the time to just love them, the upset resolves itself with peace.

Dedicated to: *The wonderful energy called love.*

Who Am I?

I am a fleeting thought in the universe,
An idea yet untried.
I am poetry in motion,

And much I've yet denied.
I am the yesterdays and
tomorrows.

I am the here and now.
Time is not of the essence.
It never was, I vow.

I am the rays of the sunshine,
The sparkling of the pool.
I am the workings of genius,

The smiles of the fool.
I am here and there and everywhere,
That I could ever find.

I am everything
I'll ever know,
The essence of my mind.

I am the rugged path I take, and
The smooth and easy way.
I am everything I listen to, everything I say.

I am the love I hear,
the love I see.
I am the love I am and evermore will be.

Today's comment: My understanding of myself became more abstract and broader. Yet, clearer. I began to go beyond the limitations of my youth and what I had been taught. My self-image was no longer a destructive energy against me. I could create boundaries for myself, or chose to have none.

Dedicated to: *All the moments we have met on the abstract levels of life and have forgotten to bring it back into our consciousness.*

I AM

I am a Child of God called woman.
I am my own creation - all I want to be.

I am the flowing of a fountain.
    I am love eternally.

I am the softness of a rose petal.
    I am the vintage of good wine.

I am the pleasure of a rainbow.
    I am the joy of love divine.

I am the vastness of the Universe.
    I am the flower in the wild.

I am as gentle as a wind song.
    I am the innocence of a child.

I am the beauty of a sunset.
    I am the freedom of eternity.

Today's comment: I began to seek for my oneness with all things. I began to find connections everywhere. Everything I looked at began to reflect to me, the love that I allowed to flow from me. Everything became more beautiful.

Dedicated to: *The energy called will. The willingness to move forward in my life even though I couldn't see where it was taking me. The willingness to take a chance. The willingness to believe that what I didn't know could be better than what I did know.*

Changes

The changes have been many and
     I wasn't even aware of most of them,
         Yet, they were almost drastic.

The personality changes were evident
     with each physical change of
         the many people I've been.

What did it all mean?
     How could one person go through
         so many changes and conflicts within?

The inner conflict was as much a part
     of each change as the physical
         and the personality changes.

Always, there was a search going on
     deep within; a restlessness that
         I did not understand.

The changes were often clumsy and painful.
     Sometimes filled with stress
         and a great deal of resistance.

The changes have not stopped, they
     have only become
         A smoother form of a natural evolution.

The changes have become
     A continuing metamorphosis
         of beauty and of grace.

Today's comment: A willingness to change made the transition much more comfortable than it otherwise would have been. When I resist change, there is always pain. When I just go with the flow of it, it is almost effortless.

Dedicated to: *Every person who has gone through or is going through a metamorphosis of their being. I acknowledge the courage it takes. Congratulations!*

ME

I am like the butterfly.
Through my metamorphosis
I have gone from creature of illusion to truth -
a Child of God.

Now, I soar like an eagle,
I dare to fly.
For my wings are
the wings of love.

As I fly through the Universe,
I touch each star
and leave with it
a part of myself.

I pour forth love from my being,
for I shall not pass this way again.
Tomorrow doesn't exit.
Yesterday is only an illusion.

There is only this moment – now.
To love and to be loved.
To give and receive.
To forgive and be forgiven.

There is only this moment.
To love you.
To love myself.
To be one in God.

Today's comment: A new woman. A new image. My life began to unfold. I can't say that I always recognized the unfoldment until later when I looked back, but it was very definitely there.

Dedicated to: *New perceptions. My, how they can change one's life!*

The Art Of Life

My life is a canvas. I am an artist.
I paint with feelings, thoughts and ideas,
always creating something new.
My painting is never finished.

Somedays, I'm beautiful.
Somedays, I'm stormy.
Somedays, I'm soft or quiet.
Somedays, I'm the sunrise or the sunset.

As the colors flow and mix, my life changes.
Always I am experimenting and trying new colors.
Maybe today I'll paint with emotion, tomorrow with ideas.
Maybe I'll even blend both together to see what I get.

If I don't like what I've painted, I can paint over it.
I can change the color scheme
Or the scenery to fit my mood
just by changing what I think.

I can be all that I want to be,
or part of all that I am.
I can boldly splash my canvas with vitality,
or I can brush it subtly with hues of mellow.

I can pour upon it in a torrent of tears
as I paint with heartache.
Or I can paint beautifully bright
in the colors of love.

Each day, I am a new masterpiece to be displayed in the
Ever changing gallery of, "The Universe."
Enjoy this painting with the realization that
knowing you has helped to create what I am.

Today's comment: Being open to life allowed it to flow with much more grace. I look back at the woman I was, and I look at the growth I have traveled through, and I can't believe they are the same woman.

Dedicated to: *The words which allow me to creatively share my life with you. Through some small chance you may find a few words here and there which will open new doorways for you on your own journey.*

A New Experience With A Man

You came into my life
like a gentle breeze
on a warm sunny day.

You touched me so softly
I could not help but
lift my very being up to you.

There passed between us a
very high energy
that seemed related to truth.

You seemed trustworthy and
I began to trust you.
My trust has turned to love.

The moments of love and joy
that I've had with you
have made me very happy.

My love for you is strong
enough for me to say,
"I'll promise you today."

I'm aware that tomorrow
is only an illusion, and
today is all there is.

So, to promise you more
than this moment in time
would be unrealistic.

In this moment I am totally
committed to you and
our love is all I know.

Today's comment: I met this man in 1983. We've been married for 37 years.

Dedicated to: *Allen Ogden, the wonderful man I continue my journey with.*

The Gift

You are so beautiful,
I wanted to give you a gift of love.

I tried to think of something valuable.
Nothing came to mind.

I began to think about what I would want to receive.
What I came up with, I couldn't buy.

I decided that if it meant so much to me
that it might also mean a lot to you.

So, my gift to you is
My unconditional love.

To let you know that when you are happy,
my face shines with your laughter.

When you are troubled
My heart feels your concern and need.

When you are sad
My eyes reflect your tears.

My gift is my total self,
To share your happiness, your tears, your joy and fears.

I give you all that I am,
To use for strength, courage, and love.

I'll always be there when you need
a helping hand or a listening ear.

Or just someone to share your own being
with, no matter what you are being.

Today's comment: I made this commitment to Allen long ago, and I still live by it today.

Dedicated to: *Allen. He has loved me through all kinds of growth. He has always encouraged me to be all that I can be. Giving is truly receiving.*

Love - A Wonderful Flight

You are a song in my heart.
　　You play my tune to perfection.
　　　　Revealing depths of myself I
　　　　　　Had been totally unaware of

You have drawn from me a sensitivity
　　That is vibrantly alive, yet
　　　　Softly caresses my very being.
　　　　　　You lift my spirit to heights previously unknown.

Layer by layer, you've removed the veils
　　I had carefully stretched o'er my existence.
　　　　I'm drawn but withdrawn. I wait.
　　　　　　I've Been touched with love. My senses are alive.

The intensity of love has entered my life.
　　I am blinded no longer. I see love
　　　　as wings with which I can soar on high.
　　　　　　I accept love -- A wonderful flight.

Today's comment:　　When one learns selflove, the dance of love with another is based upon, beauty, trust, joy, sharing, laughter, and lots and lots of hugs.

Dedicated to: *Allen Ogden - the sweetest man I know.*

To My Loving Allen

In a time when life was hard
God answered my
prayers and
sent an angel to help me and love me.

    Through that angel's
    constant love and
    acceptance my life
    changed.

        The struggles of
        life became the
        chapters of a life
        long gone.

Victim ship and
anger, literally,
slipped through
my grasp.

    Love began to work,
    and as it grew within me,
    I became a new woman,
    once again.

        Softness and gentleness
        replaced the old angers and
        resentments as our life,
        together began to unfold.

Loving myself and
seeing that I
had value
was very enlightening.

    Loving others became
    so much easier to do
    through the light that
    I now allowed.

        It is my heart's belief
        that you are the angel
        God sent to me.
        I love you, Allen

Love Is Worth The Risk It Takes To Have

Love is worth the work it takes to have.

Love is worth the heartache it takes to let go of.

Love is worth the change it requires of us.

Love is worth letting go of old pain.

Love is worth the self-discipline it requires.

Love is worth re-evaluating our belief systems.

Love is worth holding out for.

Love is who we are.

Love heals.

Love Is.

You are Love.

I am Love.

Let us heal the world, together.

Billie

Embrace Love

My friends, embrace your journey,
while loving
Yourself, and all others.

You will find your world changing
for the better and
for the good of all.

Close your eyes.
Now allow Universal Love
to flow through you.

Know that I am sending Love to you,
Right Now!
Accept it! • Embrace it! • Bathe in it!

My prayers are
that you will find
yourself within yourself.

Embrace Love
Billie

Where Did Thirty-Seven Years Go?

It feels like yesterday that you called my office
and asked me to have lunch with you.
We spent two hours telling each the
very worst things about ourselves.

    I went back to my office and
    my secretary asked me, "Well?"
    I grinned and said, "I am going to marry that man."

Within two months, we decided it was logical to move in together,
considering we both had to find new living quarters.
It saved us both money to do so.

    For a year and a half, we had a good life together,
    And enjoyed each other's company.
    I fell in love, but you decided to move to Seattle.

My heart felt broken.
I felt broken all-over, again.
It took me a while to find myself, but I did.

    Five months later, you called and asked me to marry you.
    I asked you if it was to be a closed marriage, you said yes.
    I also said yes.

We married in Seattle and made it our home.
We began our Spiritual path together. I channeled, saw clients and did workshops.
You worked as an accountant. We made God our Spiritual focus.

    We felt spiritually adventurous,
    so, we backpacked from Katmandu, Nepal to Lhasa, Tibet,
    then traveled through Thailand and across China on our way home.

We moved to Sagle Idaho; spent 23 years tending our fifteen beautiful acres.
Within that time, we spent a year in Fairfield Iowa.
You worked as an accountant/truck-driver and I as a Metaphysical Consultant.

    We laughed together, cried together, supported each other, loved each other,
    listened to each other, worried together, solved problems together
    and held hands through it all. We are still holding hands.

Thirty-seven years go by very quickly
when you spend it with someone you love and respect
and cherish each moment you have together.

Billie shortly after her divorce from her first husband and before she met Allen

Billie Stephens 1981

Billie and Allen met at a portable computer manufacturer in Solana Beach California in 1983 and moved in together within a month after they met.

Billie Stephens and Allen Ogden 1983

Billie and Allen married in 1985. After 37 years of marriage, they both insist that their love, admiration, and enjoyment of each other's company is greater than when they were first married. They are still holding hands.

Billie Stephens-Ogden And Allen Ogden 2022

About the Book

This book was written for those who find themselves inadequate and alone to meet life's challenges, with little or no support; having only themselves to count on. That is how the author found herself after her divorce. She began writing a journal which enabled her to express her thoughts and activities, which gave her hope.

The journal became the source for this book. The trauma of her life forced her to turn within, where she found answers. What she learned is **"All things work together for good.**

HOWEVER, that phrase comes with a caveat:
> It requires that we fully believe and KNOW there is a power, greater than our finite selves, and we are an expression of this omnipotent, omniscient, and omnipresent source. **The journey requires the Will to be the best we can be.**

What the author has learned, is how, through life's trials and tribulations, successes, and failures, we can choose to turn within for the answers. As we become more and more aware that there is indeed a power greater than the finite, we evolve into something greater. This does not happen over-night. We must be vigilant in watching our thoughts. Evolution to realms of higher being takes time. We are all capable.

You will find throughout this book, that the author has her ups and downs, successes and failures, but through her persistent belief in the higher power within us, she found so much more than she hoped for, both within and without. She was able to do this and so can you. Love is not a relationship per se, it is the energy that is put into a relationship. It requires us to see our Oneness within and through all things. It takes letting go of fear and embracing love.

Printed in the United States
by Baker & Taylor Publisher Services